INVEST KIDS™

BALANCING A CHECKBOOK

Gillian Houghton

PowerKiDS press™

New York

Published in 2009 by The Rosen Publishing Group, Inc.
29 East 21st Street, New York, NY 10010

First Edition

Editor: Joanne Randolph
Book Design: Julio Gil
Photo Researcher: Jessica Gerweck

Photo Credits: Cover © Kevin Hatt/Getty Images; back cover, pp. 10, 14, 17 Shutterstock.com; p. 5 © Jayme Thornton/Getty Images; p. 6 © Jason Dewey/Getty Images; p. 9 © Jon Riley/Getty Images; p. 13 © Bruce Ayres/Getty Images; p. 18 © Eric Larrayadieu/Getty Images; p. 21 © Mark Romine/age fotostock.

Library of Congress Cataloging-in-Publication Data

Houghton, Gillian.
  Balancing a checkbook / Gillian Houghton. — 1st ed.
      p. cm. — (Invest kids)
  Includes index.
  ISBN 978-1-4358-2772-1 (library binding) — ISBN 978-1-4358-3207-7 (pbk.)
ISBN 978-1-4358-3213-8 (6-pack)
  1. Checking accounts—Juvenile literature. I. Title.
  HG1691.H68 2009
  332.024—dc22
                                    2008037755

Manufactured in the United States of America

Contents

Getting Started

Do you know how much money you have in your piggy bank? Have you ever counted it all up? If you do not know how much you have, you do not know how much you can spend. Maybe it is time to start keeping track of how much money you earn, spend, and save. It is time to learn about checking **accounts**! When you have a checking account, you write down all the money you put into your account and all the money you take out of it.

Many banks will not let you open a checking account until you are 16 years old. Until then, you can practice banking at home. All you need is a piece of paper and a pencil!

To practice having a checking account, count what you have saved and write it down on a piece of paper. Every time you add money or take money out, be sure to write it down.

This man is writing out a check at a bank. He will give the check to the bank teller and the teller will give him cash from his account.

What Is a Checking Account?

A bank is a **business** that offers many different services to its **customers**. Bank customers may borrow money from banks, or they may open up a savings or checking account. Many bank customers pay to keep their money in checking accounts. A checking account is an account that lets you **withdraw** money to make a **payment** using a check or a debit card.

A check is a piece of paper issued, or given out, by the bank. A debit card is a piece of plastic that works like a credit card. Checks and debit cards are easier and safer to carry than cash.

How Do Checking Accounts Work?

When you open a checking account, the bank gives you an account number. This number is just for your account. This way, the bank knows where to put deposits and from which account to withdraw money when you write a check. The account number is printed on every check you use, along with a number that stands for the bank where the account is held.

You must **deposit** money into your account so that it will be there to withdraw when you need it. When you use a check, you agree to let your bank withdraw a certain amount from your account and give it to the payee, or the person to whom you gave the check.

This woman is opening up a checking account at a bank. She can make payments and take out cash from the account, while the rest of her money stays safely in the bank.

2007			2008			2009		

2007

JANUARY	FEBRUARY	MARCH
S M T W T F S	S M T W T F S	S M T W T F S
1 2 3 4 5 6	1 2 3	1 2 3
7 8 9 10 11 12 13	4 5 6 7 8 9 10	4 5 6 7 8 9 10
14 15 16 17 18 19 20	11 12 13 14 15 16 17	11 12 13 14 15 16 17
21 22 23 24 25 26 27	18 19 20 21 22 23 24	18 19 20 21 22 23 24
28 29 30 31	25 26 27 28	25 26 27 28 29 30 31

APRIL	MAY	JUNE
1 2 3 4 5 6 7	1 2 3 4 5	1 2
8 9 10 11 12 13 14	6 7 8 9 10 11 12	3 4 5 6 7 8 9
15 16 17 18 19 20 21	13 14 15 16 17 18 19	10 11 12 13 14 15 16
22 23 24 25 26 27 28	20 21 22 23 24 25 26	17 18 19 20 21 22 23
29 30	27 28 29 30 31	24 25 26 27 28 29 30

JULY	AUGUST	SEPTEMBER
1 2 3 4 5 6 7	1 2 3 4	1
8 9 10 11 12 13 14	5 6 7 8 9 10 11	2 3 4 5 6 7 8
15 16 17 18 19 20 21	12 13 14 15 16 17 18	9 10 11 12 13 14 15
22 23 24 25 26 27 28	19 20 21 22 23 24 25	16 17 18 19 20 21 22
29 30 31	26 27 28 29 30 31	23 24 25 26 27 28 29
		30

OCTOBER	NOVEMBER	DECEMBER
1 2 3 4 5 6	1 2 3	1
7 8 9 10 11 12 13	4 5 6 7 8 9 10	2 3 4 5 6 7 8
14 15 16 17 18 19 20	11 12 13 14 15 16 17	9 10 11 12 13 14 15
21 22 23 24 25 26 27	18 19 20 21 22 23 24	16 17 18 19 20 21 22
28 29 30 31	25 26 27 28 29 30	23 24 25 26 27 28 29
		30 31

2008

JANUARY	FEBRUARY	MARCH
S M T W T F S	S M T W T F S	S M T W T F S
1 2 3 4 5	1 2	1
6 7 8 9 10 11 12	3 4 5 6 7 8 9	2 3 4 5 6 7 8
13 14 15 16 17 18 19	10 11 12 13 14 15 16	9 10 11 12 13 14 15
20 21 22 23 24 25 26	17 18 19 20 21 22 23	16 17 18 19 20 21 22
27 28 29 30 31	24 25 26 27 28 29	23 24 25 26 27 28 29
		30 31

APRIL	MAY	JUNE
1 2 3 4 5	1 2 3	1 2 3 4 5 6 7
6 7 8 9 10 11 12	4 5 6 7 8 9 10	8 9 10 11 12 13 14
13 14 15 16 17 18 19	11 12 13 14 15 16 17	15 16 17 18 19 20 21
20 21 22 23 24 25 26	18 19 20 21 22 23 24	22 23 24 25 26 27 28
27 28 29 30	25 26 27 28 29 30 31	29 30

JULY	AUGUST	SEPTEMBER
1 2 3 4 5	1 2	1 2 3 4 5 6
6 7 8 9 10 11 12	3 4 5 6 7 8 9	7 8 9 10 11 12 13
13 14 15 16 17 18 19	10 11 12 13 14 15 16	14 15 16 17 18 19 20
20 21 22 23 24 25 26	17 18 19 20 21 22 23	21 22 23 24 25 26 27
27 28 29 30 31	24 25 26 27 28 29 30	28 29 30
	31	

OCTOBER	NOVEMBER	DECEMBER
1 2 3 4	1	1 2 3 4 5 6
5 6 7 8 9 10 11	2 3 4 5 6 7 8	7 8 9 10 11 12 13
12 13 14 15 16 17 18	9 10 11 12 13 14 15	14 15 16 17 18 19 20
19 20 21 22 23 24 25	16 17 18 19 20 21 22	21 22 23 24 25 26 27
26 27 28 29 30 31	23 24 25 26 27 28 29	28 29 30 31
	30	

2009

JANUARY	FEBRUARY	MARCH
S M T W T F S	S M T W T F S	S M T W T F S
1 2 3	1 2 3 4 5 6 7	1 2 3 4 5 6 7
4 5 6 7 8 9 10	8 9 10 11 12 13 14	8 9 10 11 12 13 14
11 12 13 14 15 16 17	15 16 17 18 19 20 21	15 16 17 18 19 20 21
18 19 20 21 22 23 24	22 23 24 25 26 27 28	22 23 24 25 26 27 28
25 26 27 28 29 30 31		29 30 31

APRIL	MAY	JUNE
1 2 3 4	1 2	1 2 3 4 5 6
5 6 7 8 9 10 11	3 4 5 6 7 8 9	7 8 9 10 11 12 13
12 13 14 15 16 17 18	10 11 12 13 14 15 16	14 15 16 17 18 19 20
19 20 21 22 23 24 25	17 18 19 20 21 22 23	21 22 23 24 25 26 27
26 27 28 29 30	24 25 26 27 28 29 30	28 29 30
	31	

JULY	AUGUST	SEPTEMBER
1 2 3 4	1	1 2 3 4 5
5 6 7 8 9 10 11	2 3 4 5 6 7 8	6 7 8 9 10 11 12
12 13 14 15 16 17 18	9 10 11 12 13 14 15	13 14 15 16 17 18 19
19 20 21 22 23 24 25	16 17 18 19 20 21 22	20 21 22 23 24 25 26
26 27 28 29 30 31	23 24 25 26 27 28 29	27 28 29 30
	30 31	

OCTOBER	NOVEMBER	DECEMBER
1 2 3	1 2 3 4 5 6 7	1 2 3 4 5
4 5 6 7 8 9 10	8 9 10 11 12 13 14	6 7 8 9 10 11 12
11 12 13 14 15 16 17	15 16 17 18 19 20 21	13 14 15 16 17 18 19
18 19 20 21 22 23 24	22 23 24 25 26 27 28	20 21 22 23 24 25 26
25 26 27 28 29 30 31	29 30	27 28 29 30 31

1028

DATE

PAY TO THE ORDER OF _____ $

DOLLARS

Security Features Details on Back

FOR _____

⑆22222222⑆ 000 111 555⑈ 1028

Do you see the places on this check for the date, the payee's name, and the amount? You write the amount as a number in the white box and as words on the line below.

Paying by Check

The first step in filling out a check is to write the date in the space at the top right corner. Next, write the name of the payee on the long line after the words "pay to the order of." Next to the payee's name, write the amount of the payment in numbers. Then write the dollar amount of the payment in words, followed by the cents written as a **fraction**.

Beside the word "memo" or "for," write what you bought using this check. The memo line is meant to be used as a reminder. Finally, sign the check in the lower right corner.

Follow That Check!

Your grandmother sent you a check for $20 for your birthday. After you write her a thank-you note, you take the check to the bank. You hand the check to the bank teller and he gives you a new $20 bill. Have you ever wondered where the check goes next?

Your grandmother's check, along with thousands of others, is sent to a **check processing center**. There, the checks are sorted and grouped together based on which bank issued them. Your grandmother's bank pays your bank $20. Her bank then withdraws the money from her account.

Your grandmother opened a checking account at her neighborhood bank. The bank near you can cash the check because the data about her bank is printed on her check.

Ask your father to show you his bank statement when he looks at it on the computer or when it comes in the mail. He can show you how it matches his check register, too.

Keeping Track

When you have a checking account, your bank will send you a letter called a statement every month. This is a list of all your transactions, or deposits and withdrawals, for the month. Every statement will tell you your balance, or the amount of money left in your account at the end of the month, too.

Do not wait for the statement to come each month. You should be keeping track of your transactions in your **check register**. This is a small notebook that comes with your checks. In it, write down the important **information** about each transaction.

Add It Up!

Every time you make a deposit to your account, make a note of it in your check register. First, write the date. Under "transaction," write "deposit." Under the heading "deposit" or "credit," write the amount in numbers. The dollar amount goes to the left of the center line, and the number of cents goes to the right of the center line.

Add the amount of your deposit to your earlier balance, which should appear under the heading "balance" in the line above. Write the new amount in numbers under the "balance" heading as well.

Do you see how this check register has lots of columns and rows? You can make your own check register on a piece of paper or ask your parents if they have an extra one.

We can use checks to buy things, as this family is doing. After he pays, this man will note the check number, the name of the store, and how much he paid for his food.

Spending Money

Just as you note each deposit, you must note every withdrawal. Every time you write a check, use your debit card, or withdraw money at the bank, write down the information in your check register.

Write the date and the check number. The check number is printed in the top right corner of each check. Under the "transaction" heading, write down the payee's name. Under the "check" or "debit" heading, write the amount of money you spent. Subtract the amount of money you spent from the amount listed under "balance" from the line above. This is your new balance.

A Balancing Game

It can take a few days before the money you promise to the payee when you write a check actually gets withdrawn from your account. This is sometimes called waiting for a check to clear. During that time, you might use more checks or make deposits. In order to know whether you have enough money in your account to pay for the things you need and want to buy, you should track your balance in your check register.

When you get your bank statement in the mail each month, make sure it matches up with your check register. Make sure neither you nor your bank has made any mistakes.

It is important to keep track of what you are spending in your check register. You get a bank statement only once a month, but you may write a check every day!

Spend Smart

Spending money can be fun, but it has a serious side. You should always know how much money you have in your account and whether it will cover the check you are about to write. What happens if you do not have enough money in your account?

If you write a check for more money than you have in your account, your bank will let you **borrow** the money. The money you borrow is called an overdraft. Usually, the bank will charge you a fee, or extra money for the overdraft. You are better off knowing your balance and spending only the money that you know you have in your account.

GLOSSARY

accounts (uh-KOWNTS) Special places where a bank keeps money set aside for a person. In a checking account, this money can be taken out using a check.

borrow (BOR-oh) To use something that belongs to someone else for a certain time.

business (BIZ-nes) A company or group of people that buys, sells, or makes things.

check processing center (CHEK PRO-ses-ing SEN-ter) An office owned by the government to help banks handle checks.

check register (CHEK REH-juh-ster) A small notebook with places to write down payments and deposits that go into and out of a checking account.

customers (KUS-tuh-murz) People who buy goods or services.

deposit (dih-PAH-zut) To put into something.

fraction (FRAK-shun) A way of writing a number that shows that that number is part of a whole.

information (in-fer-MAY-shun) Knowledge or facts.

payment (PAY-ment) An amount of money to be paid to someone for a good or service.

withdraw (with-DRAW) To take out of something.

INDEX

WEB SITES

Due to the changing nature of Internet links, PowerKids Press has developed an online list of Web sites related to the subject of this book. This site is updated regularly. Please use this link to access the list:
www.powerkidslinks.com/ikids/checkbook/